T0401347

It's Time to Celebrate

HALLOWEEN

Written by
Rebecca Phillips-Bartlett

KidHaven
PUBLISHING

Published in 2026 by
KidHaven Publishing, an Imprint of
Greenhaven Publishing, LLC
2544 Clinton St., Buffalo, NY 14224

© 2025 BookLife Publishing Ltd.

Written by: Rebecca Phillips-Bartlett
Edited by: Noah Leatherland
Designed by: Ker Ker Lee

All facts, statistics, web addresses, and URLs in this book were verified as valid and accurate at time of writing. No responsibility for any changes to external websites or references can be accepted by either the author or publisher.

Cataloging-in-Publication Data
Names: Phillips-Bartlett, Rebecca.
Title: Halloween / Rebecca Phillips-Bartlett.
Description: Buffalo, NY : Kidhaven Publishing, 2026. | Series: Its time to celebrate | Includes index and glossary
Identifiers: ISBN 9781534550094 (pbk) | ISBN 9781534550100 (library bound) | ISBN 9781534550117 (ebook)
Subjects: LCSH: Halloween--Juvenile Literature | Holidays—Juvenile Literature
Classification: LCC GT4965 P45 2026 | DDC 394.2646 --dc25

Manufactured in the United States of America

CPSIA compliance information: Batch #CSKH26
For further information contact Greenhaven Publishing LLC at 1-844-317-7404.

Please visit our website, www.greenhavenpublishing.com.
For a free color catalog of all our high-quality books, call toll free 1-844-317-7404 or fax 1-844-317-7405.

Find us on

Photo Credits – Images are courtesy of Shutterstock.com. With thanks to Getty Images, Thinkstock Photo, and iStockphoto.

Recurring images – VetriciyaArt, KanKhem. Cover – KanKhem, AnastasiiaM, VetriciyaArt. 2–3 – Summer_Wind. 4–5 – Yuganov Konstantin, Alexander Raths. 6–7 – LyudmilaKa, elenafoxly, Macrovector, jennylipets, Hanaha, Viktoria Win. 8–9 – Tijana Moraca, Sean Locke Photography. 10–11 – Bondar Illia, Evgeny Atamanenko. 12–13 – Gwoeii, Natalia Kirichenko. 14–15 – Saekko, Nomad_Soul. 16–17 – Kiselev Andrey Valerevich, Monkey Business Images. 18–19 – Sean Locke Photography, Becky Wass. 20–21 – Happy Foods Tube, Aduldej, MariaTsygankova. 22–23 – Evgeny Atamanenko, Rawpixel.com.

Contents

Page 4	It's Halloween!
Page 6	The Halloween Story
Page 8	Celebrating Halloween
Page 10	Creative Corner
Page 12	Have You Seen a Witch?
Page 14	Cooking Corner
Page 16	On Halloween
Page 18	Activity Corner
Page 20	Halloween Around the World
Page 22	It's Time to Celebrate Halloween
Page 24	Glossary and Index

Words that look like <u>this</u> can be found in the glossary on page 24.

It's Halloween!

Hello! My name is Zac. Do not worry! I do not normally look like this. I am dressed up as a monster because it is Halloween! Do you like my <u>costume</u>?

Halloween is celebrated on the 31st of October every year. It is one of the world's oldest celebrations. Halloween has its roots in <u>ancient</u> times and a festival celebrated by a group of people called the Celts.

The Celts were a group of people who lived in the United Kingdom and Ireland.

The Halloween Story

Halloween is based on a Celtic festival called Samhain. This is the story of Samhain:

The Celts believed that on the night before their new year, the border between our world and the spirit world blurred. When this happened, scary creatures such as ghosts and monsters could come into our world.

On this night, the Celts celebrated Samhain to scare off the unwanted visitors. They lit big fires and wore scary masks to trick the monsters. They also left out food for the hungry creatures.

The Celts celebrated the new year in autumn.

Celebrating Halloween

Many of the ways we celebrate Halloween today are similar to the Samhain festival. The Celts wore masks to <u>disguise</u> themselves and confuse the monsters. Now, many children wear scary costumes.

Over time, Samhain became known as All Hallows' Eve, then Halloween.

The Celts left food out so the monsters would eat that rather than attack them. Now, many children visit other people's houses asking for sweets. This is called trick-or-treating.

Creative Corner

Let's Carve a Pumpkin

For Samhain, the Celts carved faces into vegetables. Now, pumpkin carving is a popular Halloween <u>tradition</u>.

You will need:

- A pumpkin
- A pen or pencil
- A sharp knife
- A grown-up

Knives are very sharp. You will need a grown-up for this activity.

How to carve a pumpkin:

1. Get a grown-up to cut a hole in the top of the pumpkin.
2. Scoop out the seeds.
3. Draw a face on the pumpkin.
4. Get a grown-up to cut the face into your pumpkin.

Have You Seen a Witch?

Many years ago, people believed witches could <u>heal</u> people. However, over time, people started to think witches were scary. People even started to believe that they could turn into cats, bats, or spiders.

The Celts believed that cats were magical. Many witches in stories have black cats as their friends. This could explain why witches and cats are such popular Halloween costumes.

Cooking Corner

Let's Bake a Black Cat Cake

You will need:

- 3/4 cup (100 g) of all-purpose flour
- 1/2 teaspoon (3 g) of baking powder
- 1 tablespoon (14 g) of cocoa powder
- 1/2 cup (100 g) of butter
- 1/2 cup (100 g) of sugar
- 2 eggs
- 1 tablespoon (15 mL) of milk
- 1/4 teaspoon (1.25 mL) of vanilla extrac
- 1 cake pan
- Parchment paper
- Chocolate frosting
- Icing or melted white chocolate

How to bake a black cat cake:

1. Heat the oven to 375 degrees Fahrenheit (190 degrees Celsius).
2. Line the pan with parchment paper.
3. Mix the ingredients together.
4. Bake for 20 minutes.
5. Wait for the cake to cool.
6. Cover your cooled cake in chocolate frosting.
7. Use melted white chocolate to give your cat cake a face.

On Halloween

Halloween starts like most other days. I go to school. At school, we sometimes do fun, spooky activities. After school, there is a Halloween party! We all wear scary costumes and have fun.

After the party, my friend's grown-up sister takes us trick-or-treating. We get lots of sweets! When I get home, I watch a scary movie with my family.

Do you like scary movies?

Activity Corner

Let's Play Apple Bobbing

Apple bobbing is a great game to play at Halloween parties. Which of your friends will win?

You will need:
- A large tub or bucket
- Some apples
- Water
- A grown-up to keep everyone safe
- People to play with

How to bob for apples:

1. Put the apples in the tub.
2. Add enough water so that the apples start to float.
3. Take turns to pick an apple out of the water. However, you can only use your mouth!

Halloween Around the World

Lots of countries all over the world celebrate Halloween in many different ways.

In Ireland, people used to celebrate Halloween with a fortune-telling bread called barmbrack. Different items were baked in the barmbrack. The item you found meant a certain thing would happen to you.

In Japan, there is a huge parade called the Kawasaki Halloween parade. Thousands of people join in.

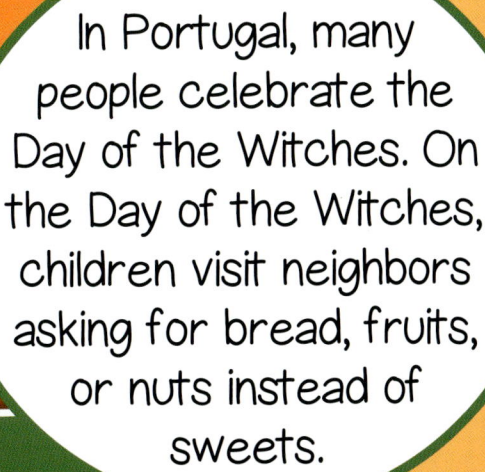

In Portugal, many people celebrate the Day of the Witches. On the Day of the Witches, children visit neighbors asking for bread, fruits, or nuts instead of sweets.

It's Time to Celebrate Halloween

You now know how Halloween is celebrated in many different parts of the world. You also know the story behind the first Halloweens and the Celtic holiday, Samhain. So, it is time to celebrate Halloween!

How will you celebrate Halloween?

You could remember how the Celts celebrated and take ideas from them. Perhaps you will make your own traditions. You could throw a spooky celebration or watch a scary movie.

Happy Halloween!

23

Glossary

ancient	belonging to the very distant past
costume	an outfit worn to look like a particular person or thing
disguise	to hide what a person really looks like, often by trying to look like someone or something else
festival	a time when people come together to celebrate a special event
heal	to make someone well again after an injury or illness
tradition	a belief or action that has been passed down between people over time

Index

apples 18–19
cakes 14–15
Celts, the 5–10, 13, 23
ghosts 6

grown-ups 10–11, 17–18
monsters 6–9
pumpkins 10–11

Samhain 6–8, 10, 13, 22
witches 12–13, 21